MAKE
YOUR OWN
SOAP

BY THE EDITORS OF KLUTZ

KLUTZ®

KLUTZ® creates activity books and other great stuff for kids ages 3 to 103. We began our corporate life in 1977 in a garage we shared with a Chevrolet Impala. Although we've outgrown that first office, Klutz galactic headquarters is still staffed entirely by real human beings. For those of you who collect mission statements, here's ours:

CREATE WONDERFUL THINGS • BE GOOD • HAVE FUN

Scent bottle, gift boxes, gift tags, boats and fish manufactured in China. Soap stickers manufactured in the USA. All other parts, Taiwan. 85

WRITE US

We would love to hear your comments regarding this or any of our books.

KLUTZ®
568 Broadway, Suite 503
New York, NY 10012
thefolks@klutz.com

Photos © Fotolia: case, cover, 28 red fish (AE.Panuwat Studio); case, front cover, title page bubble background (Volodymyr Shevchuk); box back cover (dwph).

Distributed in Australia by
Scholastic Australia Ltd
PO Box 579
Gosford, NSW
Australia 2250

Distributed in Hong Kong by
Scholastic Hong Kong Ltd
Suites 2001-2, Top Glory Tower
262 Gloucester Road
Causeway Bay, Hong Kong

ISBN 978-1-338-10645-9
4 1 5 8 5 7 0 8 8

Ingredients/Ingrédients

Soap/Savon: Water/Aqua, Sodium Cocoate, Glycerin, Sugar/Sucrose, Propylene Glycol, Sodium Palmitate, Sodium Castorate, Isostearic Acid

Dye Tablets/Comprimé Colorant: Water/Aqua, Sodium Cocoate, Glycerin, Sugar/Sucrose, Propylene Glycol, Sodium Palmitate, Sodium Castorate, Isostearic Acid, May Contain/ Peut Contenir (+/-): Red 40 Lake (CI 16035), Yellow 5 Lake (CI 19140), Blue 1 Lake (CI 42090), Titanium Dioxide (CI 77891)

Scented Oil/Huile Aromatisée: Propanediol, Linalyl Acetate, Octadecanal, Cocos Nucifera (Coconut) Oil, Ethyl Butyrate, Carica Papaya (Papaya) Fruit Extract, Butyric Acid, 2,4-Dimethyl-1,3-Dioloxane, Ethyl Propionate, Pimenta Officinalis Fruit Oil

Glitter/Brillants: Polyethylene Terephthalate, Polymethyl Methacrylate

Soap Stickers/ Tatouages: Acrylates/VA Copolymer, Shellac, Ethylcellulose, Hydroxypropylcellulose, Ricinus Communis (Castor) Seed Oil, May Contain/ Peut Contenir (+/-): Titanium Dioxide (CI 77891), Iron Oxides (CI 77499), Yellow 5 Lake (CI 19140:1), Blue 1 Lake (CI 42090:1), Red 7 (CI 15850)

Safety Notes:

Dye Tablets & Soap Stickers contain Yellow #5 which is a known irritant for people with certain sensitivities and allergies.

Warning: Scent bottle contains glass that may break.

If swallowed: Wash out mouth with water and drink some fresh water. Do not induce vomiting. Seek immediate medical advice.

CONTENTS

WHAT YOU GET

SOAP MOLD WITH 6 SHAPES

COCONUT PAPAYA SCENT

COSMETIC GRADE GLITTER

GIFT BOX

20 COLOR TABLETS

CLEAR BAG & PLASTIC FISH

GIFT TAG

20 BLOCKS OF CLEAR SOAP BASE

RIBBON

2 PAPER BOATS

SOAP STICKERS

GROWN-UPS

Please handle all heating equipment and keep an eye on your soap maker while the soap is still warm.

YOU WILL ALSO NEED

A 2-CUP (1/2 LITER) MICROWAVE-SAFE GLASS MEASURING CUP

. . . .

A CUTTING BOARD, KNIFE & RUBBING ALCOHOL IN A SPRAY BOTTLE

. . . .

A LONG-HANDLED SPOON, SPATULA, OR CHOPSTICK

HEY, GROWN-UPS!

For your safety and well-being, please read the following information carefully. There are only a few important things to remember, so we made them extra-big and easy to read.

KIDS!
Get a responsible adult assistant for all of your soap-making. Make sure they read this page, and tell them there will be a quiz at the end.

◆ Though soap-making isn't rocket science, it *is* a craft that uses hot liquids. We recommend that you, the adult, handle any materials that are being heated.

◆ The projects in this book are made with melt-and-pour soap. You will need to heat your soap in every project. Hot soap can burn if it touches your skin.

◆ Never touch the heated soap with your fingers. We recommend using a long-handled spoon or a chopstick to stir your soap or to move any plastic toys you embed in the soap.

◆ If you are sensitive to any ingredients in the coconut-papaya scented oil, you can leave your soap unscented.

◆ Use only a microwave-safe GLASS measuring cup. Do not use plastic, even if it says it's microwave-safe. The melted soap will be so hot it can melt plastic.

◆ Let your soap-making tools soak in warm water to make clean-up easier.

◆ The plastic soap mold is not microwave-safe. Never heat or microwave the soap mold.

✦✦ WARNING ✦✦
If you accidentally spill warm soap on your skin, run the affected area under cold water immediately. In case of serious burns, seek medical attention!

HOW WASHING CREATES BUBBLES

Bubbles are just pockets of air wrapped in layers of water and soap. The soap makes a kind of water sandwich (water is the filling and the soap is the bread). Soap bubbles create a sphere (ball shape) because it's the best shape to make the biggest air pocket with the smallest amount of soap and water. When the water layer gets too thin (because gravity makes water slide to the bottom, weakening the top), the bubble pops!

BASIC SOAP TECHNIQUE #1

MICROWAVE METHOD

*GROWN-UPS!
Please handle all hot equipment for this craft. Microwave your soap in bursts of only 10 seconds.

You can melt your soap base in two ways: using a microwave (shown here) or a double boiler (page 12). You can use either technique to melt the base for all the projects in this book.

Some of the color tablets look similar before they melt. Scrape a small amount with your fingernail to see the final color.

You Will Need

2+ blocks of clear soap base
(read directions for each project carefully)

2+ color tablets in color of your choice

Scent (optional)

① Place 2 blocks of soap base and 2 color tablets in a microwave-safe glass measuring cup. You may need more base depending on the project you're making. Just check the instructions.

② Put the measuring cup in a microwave, and heat for 10 seconds. Keep an eye on your soap to make sure it doesn't bubble or boil.

You can make all 7 of the soaps shown here, or up to 10 of the small soaps.

| 2 blocks | 4 blocks | 3 blocks | 2 blocks | 3 blocks | 2 blocks | 4 blocks |

3 After 10 seconds, your blocks will be a little melty, but not totally melted. That's OK! Give them a stir with a long-handled spoon or a chopstick. Add a few drops of scent, if you're using it, and stir.

4 If you still have chunks of soap, microwave them in the measuring cup for another 10 seconds, then stir. Keep going until your soap is smooth and melted and all the color is mixed in evenly.

Never heat your soap so long that it bubbles or boils.

5 Carefully pour the soap mixture into the mold of your choice. Let the soap cool for at least 30 minutes.

6 When your soap has totally cooled, turn the mold over so the soap falls out. You can gently press the back of the mold to nudge it out.

HOW DOES SOAP WORK?

soap

oil or dirt

Soap is made of teeny molecules (MOLL-ick-yools) that are way too small for you to see with your eyes. (You'll just have to take our word for it.) Each soap molecule has one end that loves water and a long tail that hates water.

When you use soap and water, the water-hating tails stick to dirt and oil. Because the water-loving ends of the soap are all pointing outward (surrounding the dirt like a bubble), they attach to the clean water, washing all that dirt away.

loves water   hates water

DOUBLE-BOILER METHOD

If you don't want to use a microwave, you can melt your soap in a double boiler.

GROWN-UPS!
You should be handling the double boiler and the stove knobs for this project.

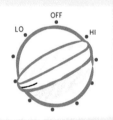

1 Add water to the bottom boiler, then place your double boiler over low to medium-low heat.

2 Place 2+ blocks of soap and an equal number of color tablets in the top boiler. Gently stir them with a spatula until they melt.

3 Add a few drops of scent if you want. Stir all the ingredients together until they blend.

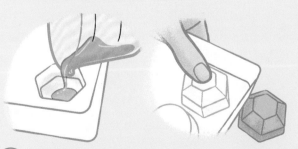

4 Follow Steps 5–6 from the microwave method on the previous page to pour, cool, and release your soap.

WHY DO YOU NEED SOAP ANYWAY?

You can't get clean with just water. Water molecules are snobby—they only like to hang out with other water molecules. If you fill a glass with water to the tippy-top, you'll see that the water surface bulges a bit above the top of the glass.

That's because water molecules pull together tightly—it's called surface tension. Water doesn't like to hang out with dirt molecules, and vice versa. You need soap, which is like the chemistry cool kid who hangs out with everyone, to mingle and wash away the dirt.

Try not to heat your soap above 160°F (70°C). Any hotter, and you may end up with rubbery soap.

GALAXY STAR

> If you see drops of liquid on your soap's surface, that's OK—it's just glycerin. Drops can appear in very humid climates, or if you put your soap in the freezer.

Glitter will make even the simplest soaps sparkle. Don't worry—the glitter will wash off your hands!

2 blocks of clear soap base

2 color tablets in color of your choice

scent (optional)

cosmetic grade glitter

1. Microwave 2 blocks of soap base and 2 color tablets for 10 seconds. Stir the blocks with a long-handled spoon. Keep microwaving 10 seconds at a time and stirring until everything is melted.

2. Add a few drops of scent and a pinch of glitter.

3. Gently stir everything with a long-handled spoon or chopstick until it's blended.

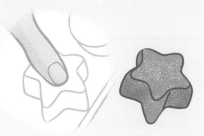

4. Pour the melted soap mixture into the star mold. It will need to cool for at least 30 minutes.

5. Turn the mold upside down to release the star soap. You can gently press the back of the mold to help it fall out.

EMOJI CAT

Soap stickers are like temporary tattoos. If you put one on your skin, it can be removed with baby oil. And if it causes irritation, be sure to remove it!

This cute soap smiles right back at ya! After you've made the soap, you'll add the soap sticker just the way you apply a temporary tattoo.

You Will Need

3 blocks of
clear soap base

scissors

3 color tablets
in color of your choice

paper towel or
clean sponge

1 soap sticker
of your choice

scent
(optional)

1 Using the cat mold, follow the instructions beginning on page 8 to create a finished piece of soap.

2 Cut out the sticker you want to use from the sticker sheet.

3 Peel off the clear plastic film from the sticker.

4 Place your soap face down on top of the sticker (this helps you check that it's centered). Flip them both over so the sticker is on top.

5 Moisten a clean sponge or a paper towel and squeeze out the extra water. Hold it on the back of the sticker, pressing down on it. Try not to get the soap wet. Moisten the back of the sticker for about 10 seconds.

6 Peel up the corner of the sticker to see if the image has stuck to the soap. If it hasn't, moisten the back of the sticker a bit longer.

SOAP-POWERED EXPERIMENTS

Try using these liquid soaps: hand soap, dish soap, laundry detergent, body wash, glycerin soap, or shampoo.

RACING BOATS

You'll find two paper boats inside the box that came with this book. Try racing them using different types of soap. Which one makes the best "fuel"?

① Float your paper boat flat on a tray of water.

② Add a dab of liquid soap in the notch on the back of the boat. Watch it zoom away!

The soap breaks up the surface tension in the water (see page 13), pushing the boat and making fireworks out of the food coloring.

FIREWORKS IN A CUP

You'll need milk, liquid food coloring, a cotton swab, and any kind of liquid soap for this activity.

① Cover the end of the swab with soap.

② Pour a small bit of milk into a cup and add drops of food coloring. Any color will work fine.

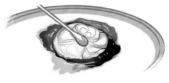

③ Place the soapy swab in the food coloring, and watch the fireworks!

PEACE SIGN

*GROWN-UPS!
Make sure to supervise your soap maker and handle all melted soap. The soap should be warm, but never too hot and never boiling.

Aah . . . This two-color soap is perfect for creating a peaceful home spa experience.

You Will Need

3 blocks of clear soap base

3 color tablets in different colors

scent (optional)

1 Melt 1 block of soap and 1 color tablet in a microwave-safe measuring cup for 10 seconds at a time. Stir between each interval. Repeat until it's all just barely melted—not too hot.

2 Add a few drops of scent, and give it all a good but gentle stir.

3 Pour the mixture into the mold to make the first layer. Try to get the colored soap only in the grooves of the peace sign.

4 Let your soap cool. Because this is a thin layer of soap, it may only take a few minutes.

5 Melt, color, and scent your next layer of soap using 2 blocks of base and 2 color tablets.

6 Pour the second color of soap into the mold, right over your first layer.

7 Once the entire soap has cooled, pop it out of the mold. If it sticks, it probably just needs to sit and cool a bit longer.

If you have a spray bottle of rubbing alcohol, you can spritz the first layer of warm soap before you add the second layer. This will help the layers stick together.

If you're giving soap as a gift, it's nice to wrap it in plastic cling to lock in the moisture.

You can go crazy with lots of layers in your soap. Be mindful that you'll only need a little bit of soap for each layer, so you'll end up with leftover soap. (You can use leftover soap to make Sprinkle Suds, page 24.)

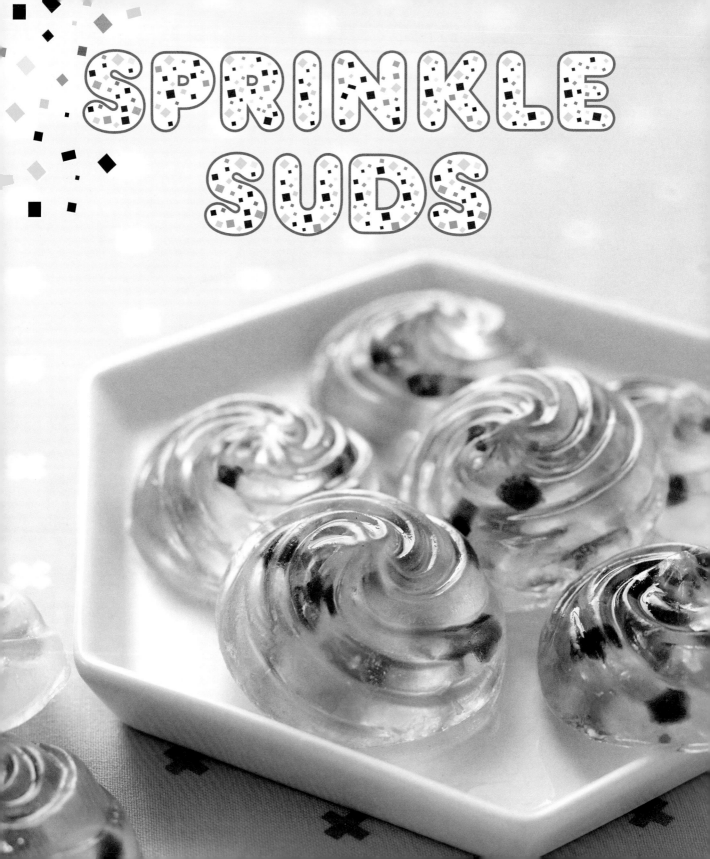

SPRINKLE SUDS

After you've washed your hands with your other soap projects, they'll eventually turn into little slivers. Recycle them into this fun and colorful soap!

1. Gather up your leftover slivers of soap from other projects in this book.

2. Have a grown-up slice up your slivers on a cutting board . . .

3. . . . then chop your slices crosswise into smaller pieces to make soap confetti.

You Will Need

Leftover soap slivers

2 blocks of clear soap base

cutting board

Knife
(grown-up needed*)

scent
(optional)

*GROWN-UPS!

The soap base is about the consistency of a block of cheese. Choose a knife that's sharp enough, and make sure that you handle all the slicing and dicing.

④ Mix up all your soap confetti.

⑤ Melt 2 blocks of clear soap base, heating 10 seconds at a time (pages 8–13). Add scent if you like. Pour half of the clear soap into the frosting mold.

⑥ Sprinkle some chopped-up soap confetti into the clear soap. Let it cool for 5 minutes.

⑦ Pour the rest of the clear soap into the mold, then add more soap confetti.

To make your soap crystal-clear, spritz your mold with rubbing alcohol before you pour in the melted soap.

⑧ Let the soap cool, then release it to reveal your finished soap.

You can even use your confetti soap to make a cupcake (page 32).
This soap also has a rainbow base (page 23).

FISHY FUN

You might just fool someone into thinking you won this at a carnival. It looks like a real fish swimming in a bag of water!

NOTE:
This project uses more soap base blocks than other projects in this book.

You Will Need

4 blocks of clear soap base

scent
(optional)

1 clear plastic bag

1 plastic fish

ribbon

1. Roll down the top of the plastic bag so it stays open and place it securely on a flat table.

2. Melt 2 blocks of soap in a microwave-safe glass measuring cup for 10 seconds at a time. Stir the blocks with a long-handled spoon or a chopstick in between microwaving, and add a few drops of scent (optional). Pour the soap into the bottom of the plastic bag.

GROWN-UPS!
Make sure the plastic bag is not in danger of falling over while you're pouring in the hot soap.

Melted soap is hot, so don't use your fingers to move the fish.

③ While the soap is still a bit warm, drop your fish into the bag. You can use your long-handled spoon or chopstick to move the fish around. Let the soap cool.

④ Melt 2 more blocks of soap in the microwave, 10 seconds at a time. Stir and add scent if you like. Pour the soap into the bag so that it covers the fish completely. Let it all cool down.

You can use this technique to embed other objects in soap. Just make sure the objects don't have any sharp edges.

⑤ Roll up the sides of the bag so it looks like it did before you started this project, and tie the ribbon around the top of the bag.

⑥ Make a bow with the ribbon, the way you would tie your shoes. It's a perfect present!

To use your fishy gift, your friend will need to unwrap the entire chunk of soap from the bag.

These **cupcake** soaps are the most complicated project in this book. Start with a simple soap (like the Galaxy Star on page 14) to get the basics down, before you try making a cupcake soap.

(like the Galaxy Star on page 14)

You Will Need

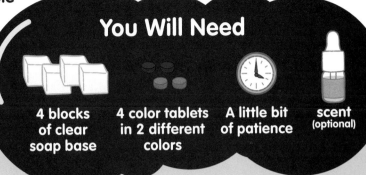

4 blocks of clear soap base

4 color tablets in 2 different colors

A little bit of patience

scent (optional)

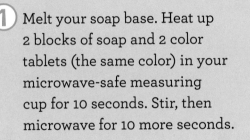

① Melt your soap base. Heat up 2 blocks of soap and 2 color tablets (the same color) in your microwave-safe measuring cup for 10 seconds. Stir, then microwave for 10 more seconds.

② Add scent, then stir until the color is blended.

③ Pour the soap into the top mold (the frosting shape).

④ Let your top cool. You may need to let it sit for an hour or even longer. When it's completely cool, pop it out of the mold. *Make sure to pop the top before you move on to Step 5.*

GROWN-UPS
Make sure to use caution while heating the soap and handling the measuring cup.

To: LIZZY

From: Caitlin

The mini dotted box that came with this book is perfect for gifting your soap creation. Just fold the bottom flaps first, add your finished soap, and tuck in the top tabs in a clockwise motion.

5 Melt 2 more blocks of soap and the other 2 color tablets, being careful to microwave them for only 10 seconds at a time.

Use only a long-handled spoon or a chopstick to mix your soapy concoction.

6 Add scent and stir until the color is nice and blended.

7 Carefully, pour the soap into the bottom mold (the base shape). Make sure the soap fills the entire mold, all the way to the top.

8 Right away, place your finished frosting top onto the warm soap in the bottom mold. The two pieces will stick together as they cool.

9 Wait for your soap to cool. Then turn it over and pop out the whole cupcake.

CREDITS

Editor: Caitlin Harpin

Designer: Kristin Carder

Technical Illustrator: Kat Uno

Photographer:
Alexandra Grablewski

Stylist: Amanda Kingloff

Package Designer:
Owen Keating

Managing Editor: Barrie Zipkin

Buyer: Vicky Eva

Cleanup Crew:
F. S. Kim, April Chorba, Armin
Bautista, and Linda Olbourne

Bubbly Personalities:
Hannah Rogge and
Netta Rabin

Cleanliness Goddess:
Stacy Lellos

P.S. Any skin-safe
temporary tattoo
will make a great
soap sticker.

Get creative with more from KLUTZ®

Looking for more goof-proof activities, sneak peeks, and giveaways? Find us online!

f Klutz Books   p Klutz Books   ▶ Klutz   ✖ @KlutzBooks   ◎ @KlutzBooks

Klutz.com • thefolks@klutz.com • 1-800-737-4123